For Mary and Maggie —A.N.

To the incomparable, inspirational, and
fabulously trailblazing Mary —B.L.

Special thanks to The Walt Disney Family Museum, whose 2014 exhibit *Magic, Color, Flair:
the World of Mary Blair* was an inspiration and an invaluable resource; to Samantha McFerrin,
Grace Lee, and Winnie Ho, for their belief in and hard work on this book; and to Mary Blair's
niece, Maggie Richardson, for her kindness, generosity, and assistance with this book

Text copyright © 2019 by Amy Novesky
Illustrations copyright © 2019 Disney Enterprises, Inc.

First Hardcover Edition, August 2019
10 9 8 7 6 5 4 3 2
FAC-034274-20233
ISBN 978-1-4847-5720-8
Printed in the United States of America
Text layout by Winnie Ho
Illustrations created with cut paper and gouache

Library of Congress Control Number: 2018042767
Reinforced binding
Visit www.disneybooks.com

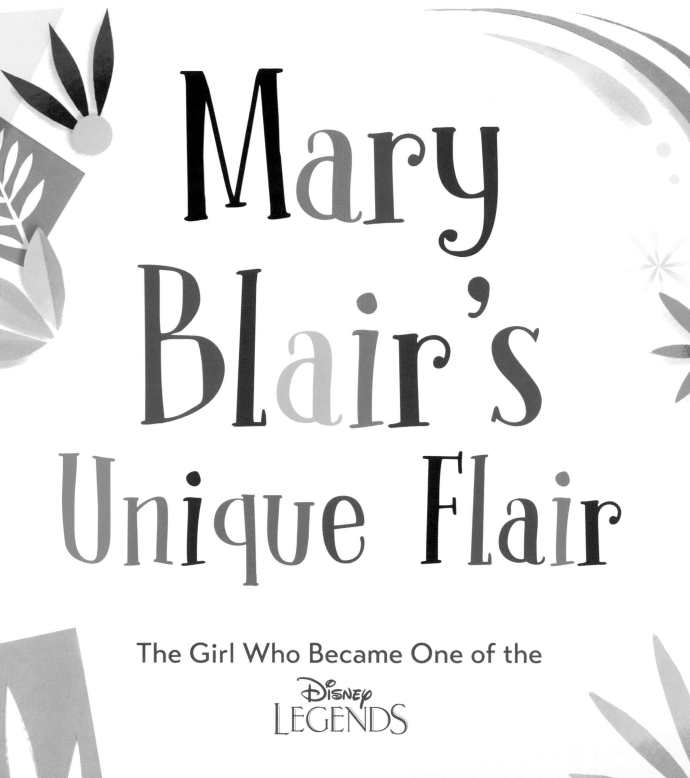

# Mary Blair's Unique Flair

## The Girl Who Became One of the

### Disney LEGENDS

Written by **Amy Novesky**

Illustrated by **Brittney Lee**

Disney PRESS

LOS ANGELES · NEW YORK

Mary Browne Robinson loved color.
Even her name had a color in it.
All she wanted was to paint.

But her family didn't have money for such things.
Still, sometimes they went with less to eat so
Mary could buy paper and jars of color.

Mary was born into an artistic home.
Her mother sewed clothing for a living.
Her father had the most beautiful handwriting—and
he was a dreamer. He dreamed of traveling.

Mary was a dreamer, too.
She dreamed of being an artist.

When the family moved from
Texas to California,
Mary carried her sketchbook
and her suitcase full of paints
all the way to the Golden State.
She loved to travel,
just like her father.

At school, Mary covered her textbooks with drawings.

She entered contests and earned a spot at a school for the arts.

She later married another artist, named Lee,
and became **Mary Blair**. They vowed to make art.
But it was hard to make a living as an artist.

So Mary took a job with the **Walt Disney Studios.**
There she painted a dog named Lady . . .

and the big emotions—and ears!—of a little elephant
named Dumbo, alongside other artists.

Despite how fun it was to work at Disney, it wasn't Mary's dream come true—yet—so she quit.
She preferred to stay home and paint.

ANIMATION

But when Mary heard that Walt was taking artists,
including Lee, on a trip to South America,
she asked Mr. Disney to take her along.

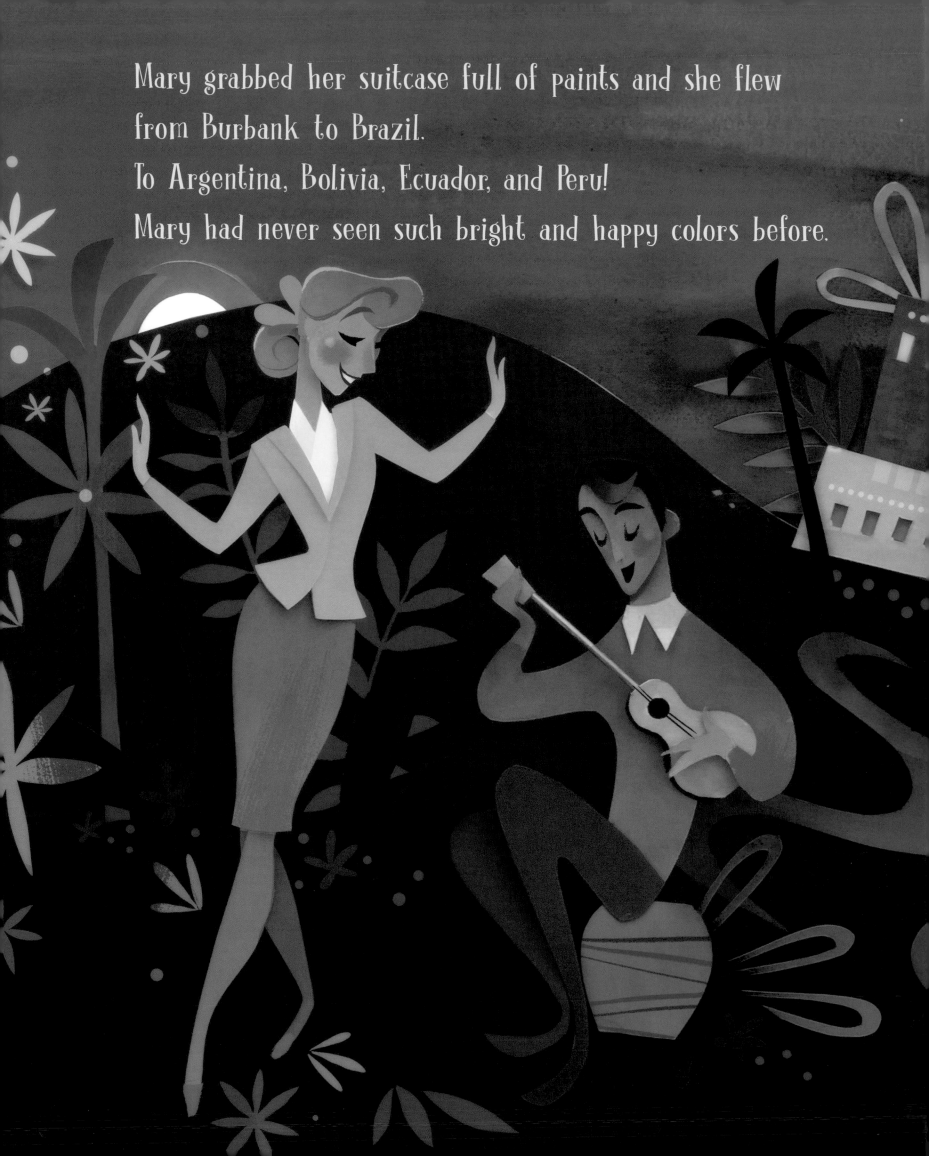

Mary grabbed her suitcase full of paints and she flew
from Burbank to Brazil.
To Argentina, Bolivia, Ecuador, and Peru!
Mary had never seen such bright and happy colors before.

Verde and azul. Amarelo,
amarillo. Laranja, anaranjado. Vermelho, rojo,
and rosa. Lilás, lavanda, roxo, morado.
Marrom, marrón. Cinza, gris, preto, negro.

And her favorite color—blanco—the color of a blank piece of paper, of possibility.

She immersed herself in the colors and the cultures—and she painted them all.

She especially loved painting the children she met.

It was a small **world** after all.

Then, with her suitcase full,

Mary went back to work for Walt.

And this time it was a dream come true.

She painted and painted.

She painted colors you weren't supposed to paint together.

Golden yellow, ocher.
Jade green and royal purple.
Hot pink and red rose madder.

She painted an iris sky.
An emerald world.
A fuchsia sea.
A turquoise moon.

Walt was a dreamer, too, just like Mary. He dreamed of making feature-length films painted entirely by hand. Nobody believed it could be done.

But Walt believed in magic,
and he believed in Mary.

So Mary painted concept art for three of Disney's most beloved animated films—

*Cinderella*...

*Alice
in
Wonderland*

Then Walt asked her, one of his favorite artists, to create
art for **a brand-new attraction at Disneyland.**
For Mary, this was the **biggest** and **best** project ever.

"It's a small world" was to feature kids from all over the world to celebrate **unity**, **goodwill**, and **global peace**.

For inspiration, all Mary had to do was open her suitcase full of paints . . .

to create colorful happily ever afters.

# From the Illustrator

Why not a fuchsia sea? An emerald world?
Wouldn't a turquoise moon be divine?
Can you imagine a silver gown made of stardust?

Mary Blair did, and her imagination soared. At once fantastic and familiar, Mary's art is magic and wonder, the stuff the best dreams are made of come to life. Once her wonderful ideas were in the world, it was hard to imagine Cinderella in anything but a dress that sparkled in the moonlight, hard to imagine a time before whimsical art like Mary's was embraced and loved by all.

I was absolutely thrilled to be asked to illustrate this book in cut paper, because working with cut paper is always a bit of an experiment. It's play. It can be tedious, but it's not too delicate to try something new. Sometimes little bits of paper come together in ways I didn't plan for, like magic. I love the surprise of it all.

When I attended an exhibit of Mary's "it's a small world" artwork at the Disney Animation Research Library a few years ago, I was shocked to discover that many of her pieces were created in cut paper! It was so exciting to see how she solved creative problems and expressed herself through colorful bits of paper and vellum. And most important, through those pieces she taught me the value of using a hole punch! Sometimes the simplest solution is the best.

The opportunity to work on this book has been my dream come true, and I hope that through these pages, readers experience the joy and inspiration Mary has given to so many. The sky, no matter what glorious color it is, is the limit!

## –Brittney Lee
Walt Disney Animation Studios

From the moment Amy Novesky came to my home to look at photos and art and listen to my stories, I knew she was someone who would understand my aunt Mary.

Mary loved and respected all children, and I treasure the memory of a long-ago visit. When I was a very young girl, I had come to see her latest project in the making—Walt Disney's now famous "it's a small world" attraction. As Mary described each land, I was dazzled by the sight of it. At one point, she turned to me and asked what color ribbon I thought should go around the long necks of a small group of geese—green or orange? I don't recall my answer, but I will never forget how special I felt when Mary asked for my opinion. That was Mary.

This wonderful book about Mary's life and work would have delighted my aunt, and it will surely delight a world of children, as well!

## –Maggie Richardson, niece of Mary Blair

Books illustrated by and books about Mary Blair include:

*A Mary Blair Treasury of Golden Books*
various authors, foreword by John Canemaker

*Alice in Wonderland*
written by Jon Scieszka

*Before the Animation Begins: The Art and Lives of Disney Inspirational Sketch Artists*
by John Canemaker

*Cinderella*
retold by Cynthia Rylant

*Ink & Paint: The Women of Walt Disney Animation*
by Mindy Johnson, foreword by June Foray

*Peter Pan*
retold by Dave Barry and Ridley Pearson

*The Art and Flair of Mary Blair*
by John Canemaker

*The Colors of Mary Blair*
Museum of Contemporary Art, Tokyo

To learn more about Mary Blair, please visit www.magicofmaryblair.com.